Your first 100 words in

PASHTO

Pashto for Total Beginners Through Puzzles and Games

Series concept
Jane Wightwick

Illustrations
Mahmoud Gaafar

Pashto edition
Akber Hargar
Akhtarjan Kohistani

Mc Graw Hill

New York   Chicago   San Francisco   Lisbon   London   Madrid   Mexico City
Milan   New Delhi   San Juan   Seoul   Singapore   Sydney   Toronto

Copyright © 2003 by Gaafar & Wightwick. All rights reserved. Printed in the United States of America. Except as permitted under the United States Copyright Act of 1976, no part of this publication may be reproduced or distributed in any form or by any means, or stored in a database or retrieval system, without the prior written permission of the publisher.

3 4 5 6 7 8 9 10 11 12 13 14 15 16 17 18 19 20 21   VLP/VLP   0 9 8 7

ISBN-13: 978-0-07-141223-0
ISBN-10:   0-07-141223-9
Library of Congress Control Number: 2004052435

McGraw-Hill books are available at special quantity discounts to use as premiums and sales promotions, or for use in corporate training programs. For more information, please write to the Director of Special Sales, Professional Publishing, McGraw-Hill, Two Penn Plaza, New York, NY 10121-2298. Or contact your local bookstore.

Other titles in this series:

Your First 100 Words in Arabic
Your First 100 Words in Chinese
Your First 100 Words in French
Your First 100 Words in German
Your First 100 Words in Greek
Your First 100 Words in Hebrew
Your First 100 Words in Italian
Your First 100 Words in Japanese
Your First 100 Words in Korean
Your First 100 Words in Persian
Your First 100 Words in Russian
Your First 100 Words in Spanish

This book is printed on acid-free paper.

◎ CONTENTS

⟳ INTRODUCTION

In this activity book you'll find 100 key words for you to learn to read in Pashto. All the activities are designed specifically for reading non-Latin script languages. Many of the activities are inspired by the kind of games used to teach children to read their own language: flashcards, matching games, memory games, joining exercises, etc. This is not only a more effective method of learning to read a new script, but also much more fun.

We've included a **Scriptbreaker** to get you started. This is a friendly introduction to the Pashto script that will give you tips on how to remember the letters.

Then you can move on to the eight **Topics**. Each topic presents essential words in large type. There is a pronunciation guide so you know how to say the words. These words are also featured in the tear-out **Flashcard** section at the back of the book. When you've mastered the words, you can go on to try out the activities and games for that topic.

There's also a **Round-up** section to review all your new words and the **Answers** to all the activities to check yourself.

Follow this 4-step plan for maximum success:

1 Have a look at the key topic words with their pictures. Then tear out the flashcards and shuffle them. Put them Pashto side up. Try to remember what the word means and turn the card over to check with the English. When you can do this, cover the pronunciation and try to say the word and remember the meaning by looking at the Pashto script only.

2 Put the cards English side up and try to say the Pashto word. Try the cards again each day both ways around. (When you can remember a card for seven days in a row, you can file it.)

3 Try out the activities and games for each topic. This will reinforce your recognition of the key words.

4 After you have covered all the topics, you can try the activities in the **Round-up** section to test your knowledge of all the 100 words in the book. You can also try shuffling all the flashcards together to see how many you can remember.

This flexible and fun way of reading your first words in Pashto should give you a head start whether you're learning by yourself or in a group.

⊚ SCRIPTBREAKER

The purpose of this Scriptbreaker is to introduce you to the Pashto script and how it is formed. You should not try to memorize the alphabet at this stage, nor try to write the letters yourself. Instead, have a quick look through this section and then move on to the topics, glancing back if you want to work out the letters in a particular word. Remember, though, that recognizing the whole shape of the word in an unfamiliar script is just as important as knowing how it is made up. Using this method you will have a much more instinctive recall of vocabulary and will gain the confidence to expand your knowledge in other directions.

Pashto, or Pakhto, is written in the Perso-Arabic script with some modified and additional characters. Reading the script is not as difficult as it might seem at first glance. There are 40 letters, no capital letters, and, unlike English, words are generally spelled as they sound. There are two main points to etch into your brain:

- Pashto is written from right to left.
- The letters are "joined up" — you cannot "print" a word as you can in English.

⊚ The alphabet

The easiest way of tackling the alphabet is to divide it into similarly shaped letters. For example, here are two groups of similar letters. The only difference between them is the dots and signs around the basic shape:

ج (the letter *jeem*)   ب (the letter *beh*)

ح (the letter *heh Arabic*)   پ (the letter *peh*)

خ (the letter *kheh*)   ت (the letter *teh*)

ځ (the letter *cheh*)   ټ (the letter *tteh*)

څ (the letter *tsee*)   ث (the letter *seh*)

ځ (the letter *zeh*)

When these letters join to other letters they change their shape. The most common change is that they lose their "tails":

$$ تج = ج + ت \qquad حب = ب + ح \text{ (read from } right to left) $$

Because letters change their shape like this, they have an *initial*, a *medial* (middle) and a *final* form. For example, the letter ج (*jeem*) changes like this:

5

at the beginning of a word (*initial*)   ‫...ج‬

in the middle of a word (*medial*)   ‫...ج...‬

at the end of a word (*final*)   ‫ج...‬

- ✔ Pashto has 40 letters and no capital letters
- ✔ Pashto reads right to left
- ✔ Pashto is written in "joined up" writing
- ✔ The "tail" is generally chopped off before joining to the next letter

A few letters change their shapes completely depending on where they fall in a word. For example, the letter ‫ه‬ (*heh*) changes like this:

initial	‫ه...‬
medial	‫...ه...‬
final	‫ه...‬

In addition, there are 10 letters which *never* join to the letter *following* (to their left) and so hardly change shape at all. These are:

‫و‬ (*waaw*)   ‫ا‬ (*alef*)

‫د‬ (*daal*)   ‫ډ‬ (*ddaal*)   ‫ذ‬ (*zaal*)

‫ر‬ (*reh*)   ‫ړ‬ (*rreh*)   ‫ز‬ (*dzeh*)   ‫ژ‬ (*zheh*)   ‫ږ‬ (*geh*)

You will find more details of how the individual letters change their shape in the table on page 8.

◎ Formation of words

We can use the principles of joining letters to form words. So, for example, the Pashto word for "hotel" is similar to English and written like this:

← ‫ه‬ (h) + ‫و‬ (o) + ‫ت‬ (tt) + ‫ل‬ (l) = ‫هوټل‬ (*hottel*)

The Pashto word for "sock" (*jooraab*), contains three non-joining letters and is written like this:

ج (j) + و (oo) + ر (r) + ا (aa) + ب (b) = جوراب (jooraab)

You may have noticed that in هوټل the *e* seems to be missing from the script. In modern Pashto, some short vowels are not written as part of the main script. It is possible to add signs above and below the script to represent these vowels, but they are not usually included in modern Pashto. So the writing is similar to English shorthand, where we might write "bnk" instead of "bank."

✔ Pashto letters have an *initial*, *medial* ("middle") and *final* form, depending on their position in the word

✔ Many Pashto letters simply lose their tails for the *medial* and *final* form

✔ A few letters change their shape completely

✔ 10 letters don't join to the letter after and hardly change at all

✔ Some short vowels are not usually included in modern Pashto

◎ Pronunciation tips

This activity book has simplified some aspects of pronunciation in order to emphasize the basics. Don't worry at this stage about being precisely correct the other letters in a word will help you to be understood.

Many Pashto letters are pronounced in a similar way to their English equivalents, but here are a few that need special attention:

ټ (*tteh*)/ ډ (*ddaal*)/ ړ (*rreh*)/ ڼ (*nneh*)	the loop below indicates an emphatic version of the letter (or nasal in the case of *nneh*). They are shown as a double letter in the pronunciation, except at the beginning of a word.
غ (*ghein*)	pronounced in the throat like the French "r" as in "rue"
خ (*kheh*)/ ښ (*kheen*)	pronounced like the "ch" in the Yiddish "chutzpah" or the German "Bach". *kheen* is pronounced as "sh" in some Pashto dialects.
ژ (*zheh*)	a soft "j," pronounced like the French "j" as in "bonjour"

A feature of Pashto is that a single sound can be represented by two or more letters, in much the same way as we can spell the sound k with either a "k" ("kettle") or a "c" ("cat"). In consequence, the sound s, for example, can be written as س, ث, or ص; and the sound z as ض, ذ, ز, غ or ظ.

There are nine letters that only appear in Arabic loan words and are relatively uncommon: ط (tweh); ظ (zweh); ص (swaad); ض (zwaad); ث (seh); ع (ain); ح (heh); ذ (zaal); ق (kaaf). Their distinctive Arabic pronunciations have disappeared in the Pashto language.

◎ Summary of the Pashto alphabet

The table below shows all the Pashto letters in the three positions, with the Pashto letter name, followed by the sound. Remember that this is just for reference and you shouldn't expect to take it all in at once. If you know the basic principles of how the Pashto script works, you will slowly come to recognize the individual letters.

	initial:	medial:	final:
alef[1]	ا	ـا	ا
beh b	بـ	ـبـ	ب
peh p	پـ	ـپـ	پ
teh t	تـ	ـتـ	ت
tteh tt	ټـ	ـټـ	ټ
seh s	ثـ	ـثـ	ث
jeem j	جـ	ـجـ	ج
heh (Arabic) h	حـ	ـحـ	ح
kheh kh	خـ	ـخـ	خ
cheh ch	چـ	ـچـ	چ
tsee ts	څـ	ـڅـ	څ
zeh z	ځـ	ـځـ	ځ
daal d	د	د	د
ddaal dd	ډ	ډ	ډ

	initial:	medial:	final:
zaal z	ذ	ذ	ذ
reh r	ر	ر	ر
rreh rr	ړ	ړ	ړ
dzeh z	ز	ز	ز
zheh zh	ژ	ژ	ژ
geh g	ږ	ږ	ږ
seen s	سـ	ـسـ	س
sheen sh	شـ	ـشـ	ش
kheen kh	ښـ	ـښـ	ښ
swaad s	صـ	ـصـ	ص
zwaad z	ضـ	ـضـ	ض
tweh t	طـ	ـطـ	ط
zweh z	ظـ	ـظـ	ظ
ain a	عـ	ـعـ	ع/عـ

	initial:	medial:	final:
ghain gh	غـ	ـغـ/ـغ	غ/ـغ
feh f	فـ	ـفـ	ف
qaaf k	قـ	ـقـ	ق
kaaf k	کـ	ـکـ	ک
gaaf g	گـ	ـگـ	گ
laam[2] l	لـ	ـلـ	ل
meem m	مـ	ـمـ	م
noon n	نـ	ـنـ	ن
nneh[3] nn	نـ	ـنـ	ڼ
waaw v/w/oo/o	و	و	و
heh h/a	هـ	ـهـ	ه/ـه
yeh[4] y/e/eh/ee	یـ	ـیـ	ی

(1) Any vowel when at the beginning of a word and also aa in medial and final positions.

(2) Note the special combination when alef is written after laam: لا, as in لاس (laas, meaning "hand").

(3) nneh never starts a word.

(4) yeh can also be written at the end of a word with additional symbols above or below, the most common of which is a final stroke: ی , which is pronounced ey, as in "hey!"

① AROUND THE HOME

Look at the pictures of things you might find in a house.
Tear out the flashcards for this topic.
Follow steps 1 and 2 of the plan in the introduction.

میز
mez

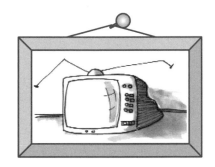

تلویزیون
talvezyoon

کرکی
karrkey

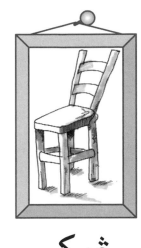

څوکی
tsawkey

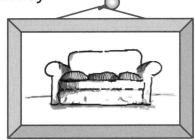

کوچ
kawch

کمپیوتر
compeotur

تیلیفون
telefoon

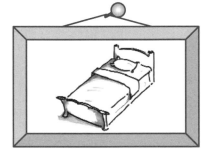

بستره کټ
bestara kutt

یخچال
yakhchaal

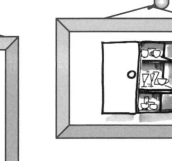

الماری
almaarey

بخاری
bokhaarey

دروازه
darwaaza

9

◎ Match the pictures with the words, as in the example.

كوچ

بستره كټ

كركى

ميز

تلويزيون

كمپيوتر

تيليفون

څوكى

- -

◎ Now match the Pashto household words to the English.

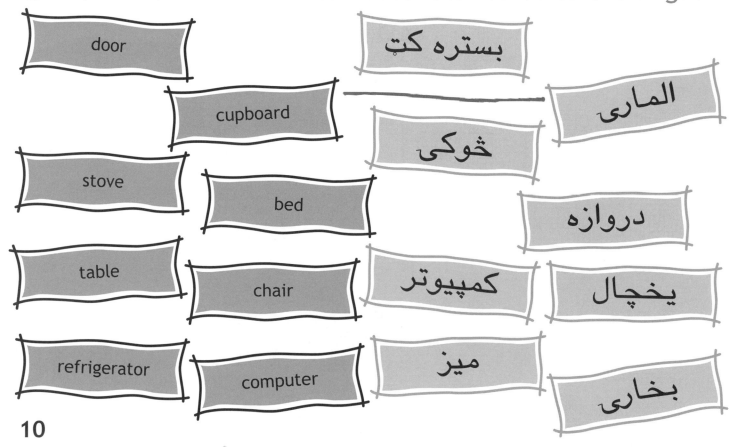

Match the words and their pronunciation.

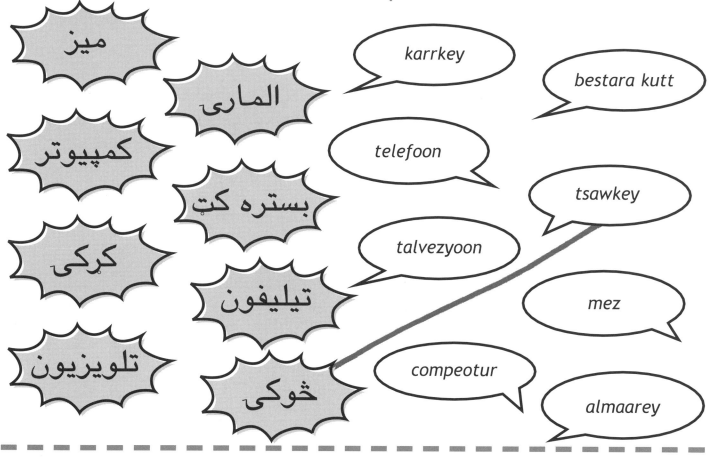

See if you can find these words in the word square.

The words run *right* to *left*.

بخاری
بستره کتہ
ژوکی
یخچال
دروازه
کوچ

ی	نـ	مـ	نـ	یـ	و	بنـ چـا
ق	گ	ه	ز	ا	ر	د
ت	بـ	پ	کـ	ل	قُ	یـ
ث	کـ	ل	ا	چـ	یـ	نـ
ت	کـ	ه	ر	ت	بـ	ژ
چ	عـ	غـ	چ	کـ	ظ	فـ
ی	رـ	ا	خـ	بـ	پ	هـ لـ
ن	یـ	بـ	یـ	و	ژژ	ش

11

⊚ **D**ecide where the household items should go. Then write the correct number in the picture, as in the example.

10 کمپیوتر	7 الماری	4 تلویزیون	1 میز
11 کړکۍ	8 بخاری	5 تیلیفون	2 څوکۍ
12 دروازه	9 یخچال	6 بستره کټ	3 کوچ

Now see if you can fill in the household word at the
bottom of the page by choosing the correct Pashto.

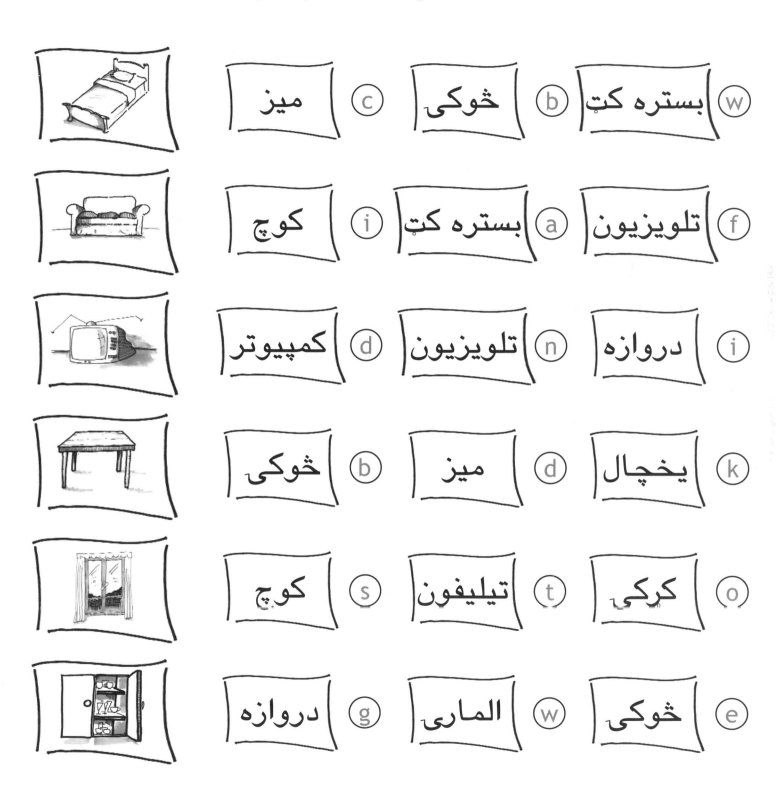

c میز	b څوکی	w بستره کټ	
i کوچ	a بستره کټ	f تلویزیون	
d کمپیوتر	n تلویزیون	i دروازه	
b څوکی	d میز	k یخچال	
s کوچ	t تیلیفون	o کرکی	
g دروازه	w الماری	e څوکی	

English word: (w) (○) (○) (○) (○) (○)

❷ CLOTHES

Look at the pictures of different clothes.
Tear out the flashcards for this topic.
Follow steps 1 and 2 of the plan in the introduction.

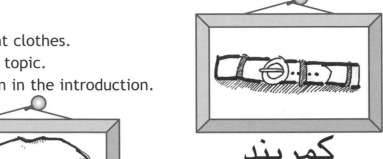

كمربند

kamarband

بنيان

banyan

نيكر

nekar

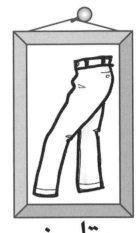

پتلون

patloon

جوراب

jooraab

كميس

kames

كرتى

kortey

لمن

laman

سخئينه
كميس

khazena kames

خولى

khowaley

بوتان

bottaan

نارينه كميس

naarena kames

14

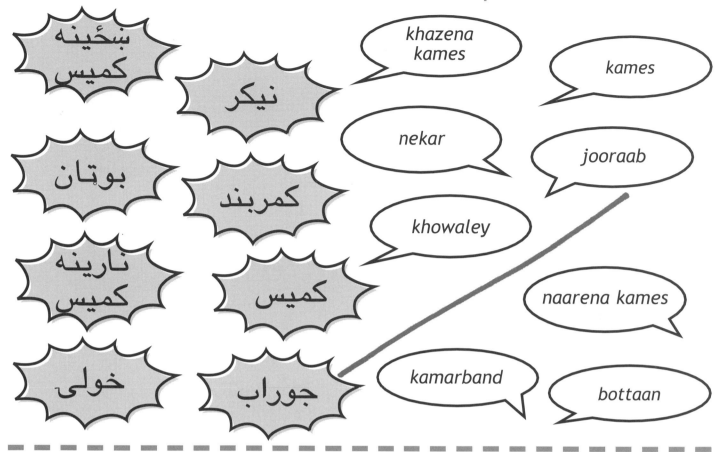 Match the Pashto words and their pronunciation.

See if you can find these clothes in the word square.

The words run *right* to *left*.

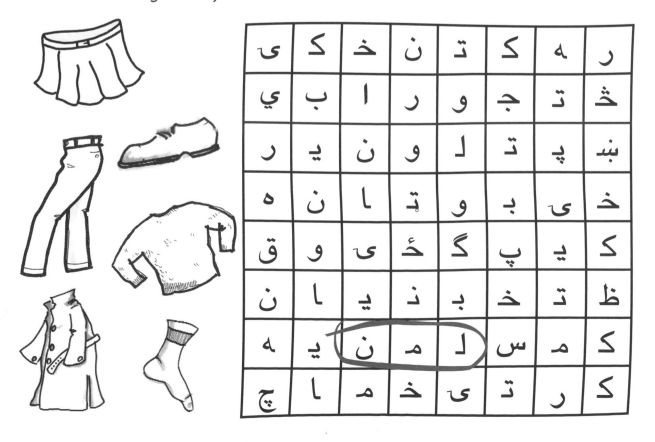

◎ **N**ow match the Pashto words, their pronunciation, and the English meaning, as in the example.

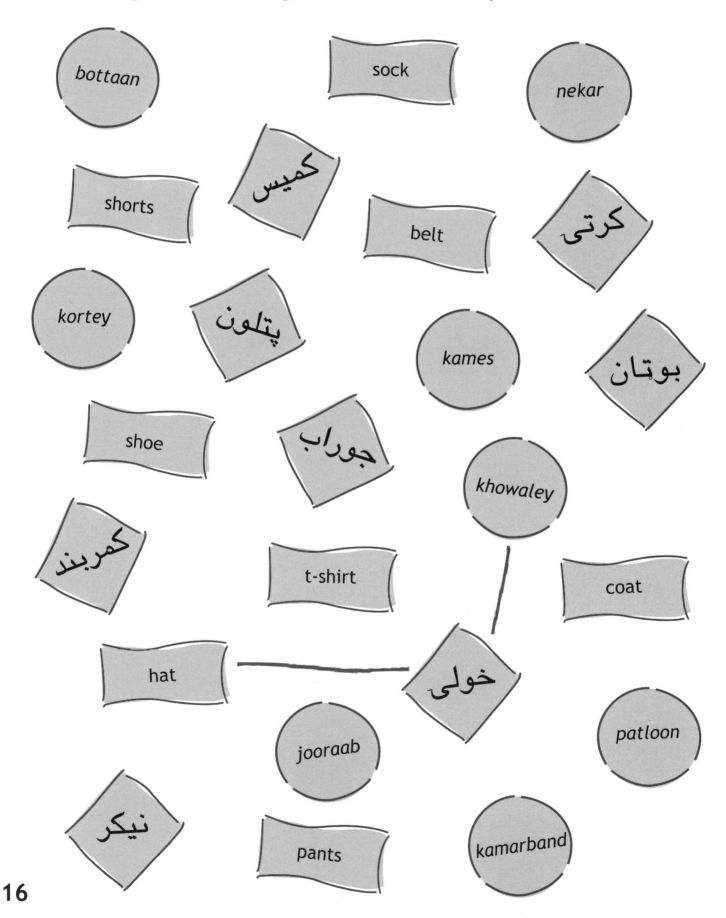

bottaan

sock

nekar

shorts

كميس

belt

كرتى

kortey

پتلون

kames

بوتان

shoe

جوراب

khowaley

كمربند

t-shirt

coat

hat

خولى

patloon

جوراب

jooraab

نيكر

pants

kamarband

Candy is going on vacation. Count how many of each type of clothing she is packing in her suitcase.

خولی ☐	کرتی ☐	کمربند ☐	بوتان 2
پتلون ☐	نیکر ☐	سپئینه کمیس ☐	جوراب ☐
لمن ☐	کمیس ☐	نارینه کمیس ☐	بنیان ☐

Someone has ripped up the Pashto words for clothes.
Can you join the two halves of the words, as the example?

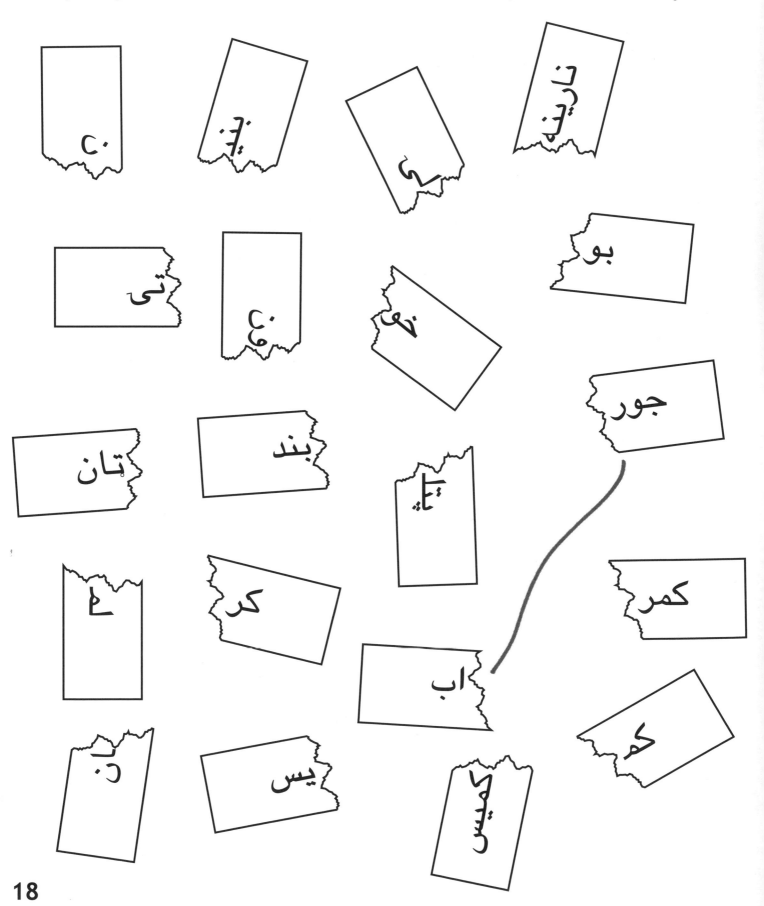

③ AROUND TOWN

Look at the pictures of things you might find around town.
Tear out the flashcards for this topic.
Follow steps 1 and 2 of the plan in the introduction.

هوتل *hottel*

سرویس
serves

کور
kor

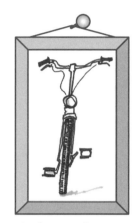

بایسکل
baaysekel

موتر
mottar

سینما
senemaa

اور گادی
or gaaddeh

تکسی *tekseh*

ښوونځی
khowanzeh

سرك *sarrak*

پلورنځی
ploranzeh

رستوران
rustoraan

◎ **M**atch the Pashto words to their English equivalents.

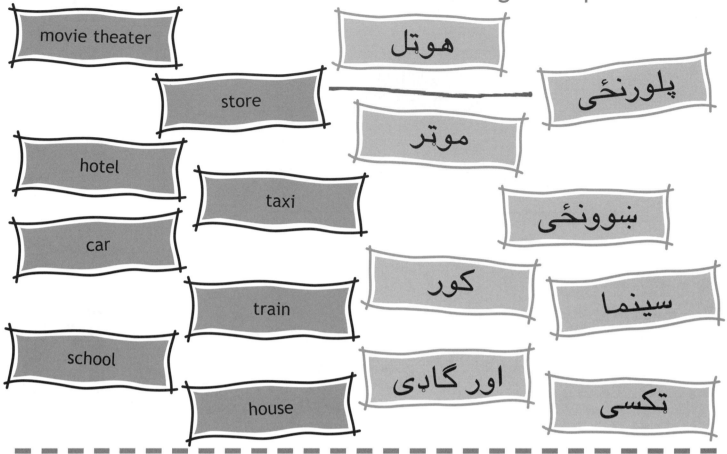

movie theater	هوتل
store	پلورنځی
hotel	موټر
car	پنځوونځی
taxi	کور
train	سینما
school	اورگاډی
house	تکسی

◎ **N**ow put the English words in the same order as the Pashto word chain, as in the example.

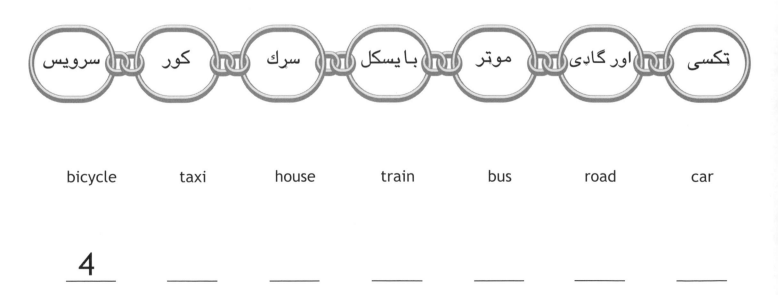

تکسی — اورگاډی — موټر — بایسکل — سرک — کور — سرویس

bicycle   taxi   house   train   bus   road   car

4 ___   ___   ___   ___   ___   ___

Match the words to the signs.

سرویس	بایسکل	موتر	بنوونځی
تکسی	هوتل	اورگادی	رستوران

Now choose the Pashto word that matches the picture to fill in the English word at the bottom of the page.

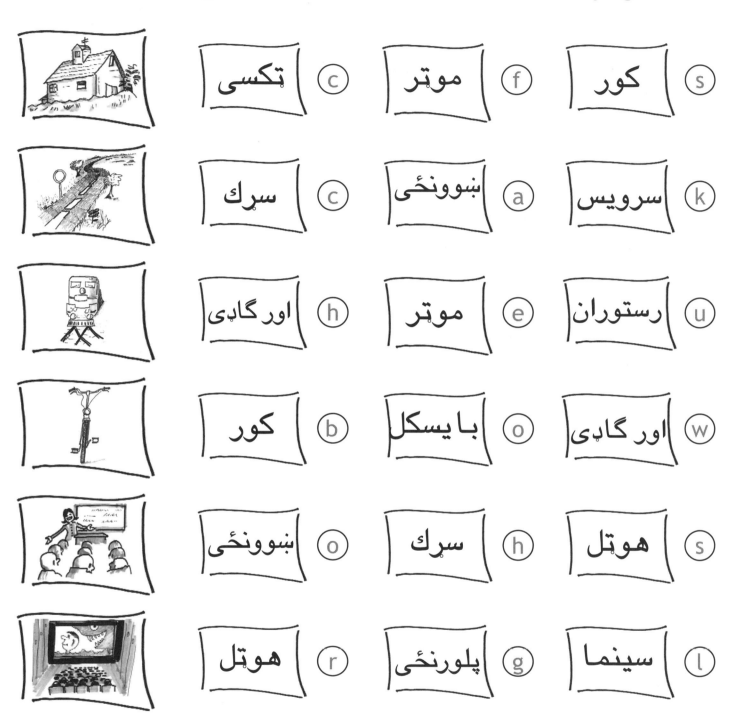

English word: (s) ( ) ( ) ( ) ( ) ( )

22

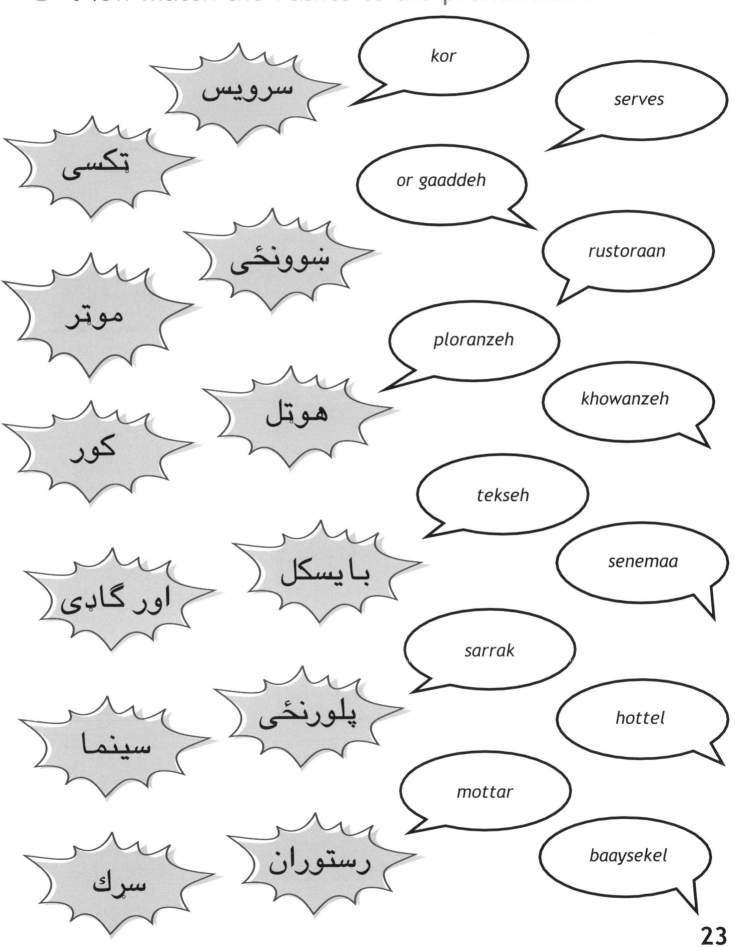

4 COUNTRYSIDE

Look at the pictures of features you might find in the countryside.
Tear out the flashcards for this topic.
Follow steps 1 and 2 of the plan in the introduction.

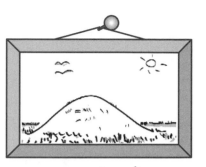

غوندی
ghonddey

پل *pul*

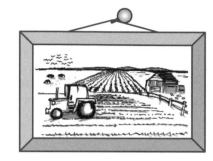

کرونده
karwanda

غر *ghar*

ډنډ *dandd*

ونه *wuna*

گل *gul*

سیند *send*

سمندر
samandar

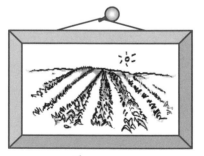

ډگر *dagar*

دبنته *dakhta*

ځنگل
zangul

Can you match all the countryside words to the pictures?

غر

کرونده

سمندر

ځنګل

دبنته

غوندۍ

بند

پل

سیند

ګل

ونه

بګر

25

Now check (✔) the features you can find in this landscape.

غوندۍ	☐	دښته	☐	ونه	☐	پل	✔
ځنگل	☐	بگر	☐	سمندر	☐	غر	☐
کرونده	☐	گل	☐	سیند	☐	بند	☐

○ **M**atch the Pashto words and their pronunciation.

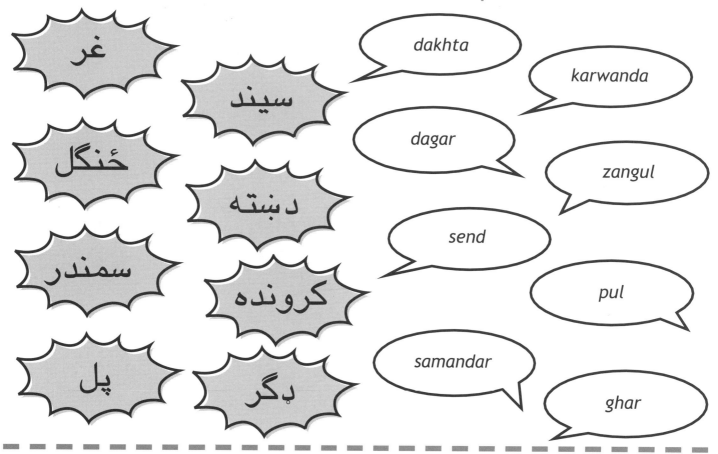

غر
سیند
خنگل
دبنته
سمندر
کرونده
پل
دګر

dakhta
karwanda
dagar
zangul
send
pul
samandar
ghar

- -

○ **S**ee if you can find these words in the word square.
The words run *right* to *left*.

ونه
کرونده
غوندی
ګل
پل
دند

ز	ظ	ی	ب	ذ	و	غ	ث
ر	ا	ب	ش	غ	م	ع	ګ
ب	ذ	ب	ت	حَ	ل	پ	ذ
ی	م	ی	بـ	ل	ګ	ل	د
چ	ه	د	ذ	و	ر	ک	ی
ت	پ	ذ	ه	و	ذ	ق	ظ
م	ه	ذ	و	ل	ع	ذ	غ
ا	ګ	پ	س	ل	ک	ع	ب

27

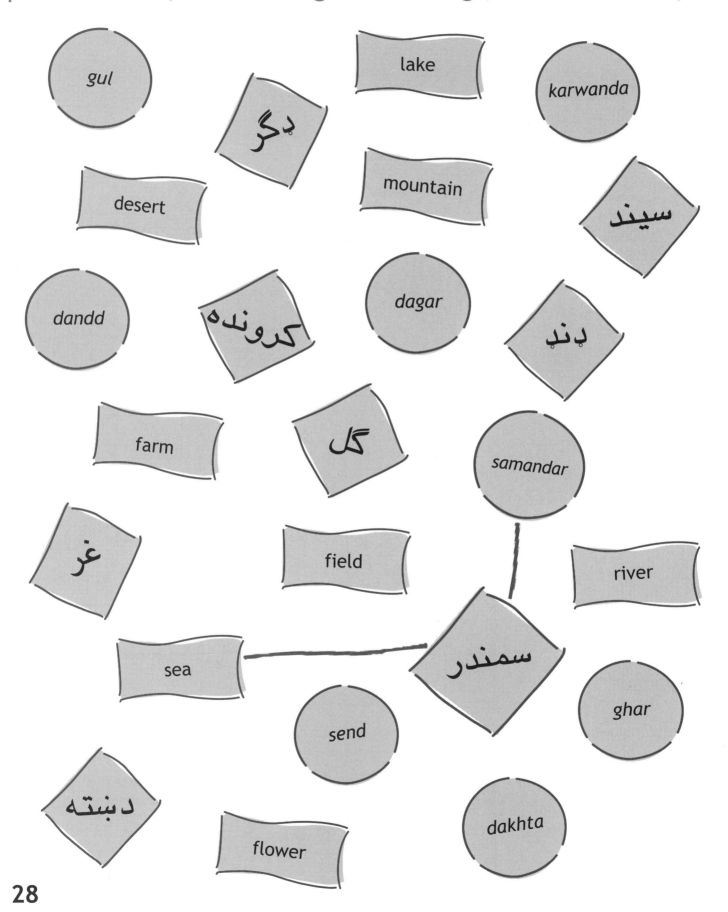

Finally, test yourself by joining the Pashto words, their pronunciation, and the English meanings, as in the example.

gul

lake

karwanda

دګر

desert

mountain

سیند

dandd

کرونده

dagar

دنډ

farm

گل

samandar

غر

field

river

sea

سمندر

send

ghar

دبنته

flower

dakhta

28

⑤ OPPOSITES

Look at the pictures.
Tear out the flashcards for this topic.
Follow steps 1 and 2 of the plan in the introduction.

چتل
chattel

پاک *paak*

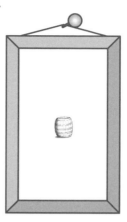

کوچنی
kochneh

لوی
luwee

ارزانبیه
arzaanbaya

سپک *spak*

ورو *wro*

لوربیه
lowarrbaya

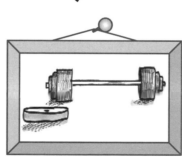

دروند *droond*

تیز *teaz*

زور *zoorr*

نوی *naweh*

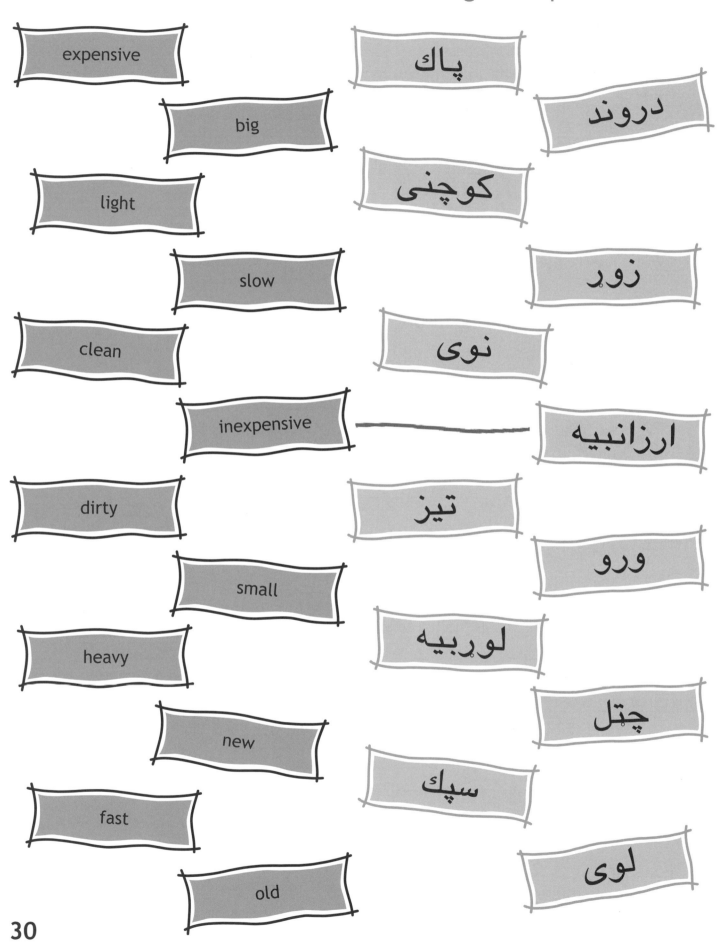

expensive

پاك

big

دروند

light

كوچنى

slow

زور

clean

نوى

inexpensive ———————— ارزانبيه

dirty

تيز

small

ورو

heavy

لوربيه

new

چتل

fast

سپك

old

لوى

30

Now choose the Pashto word that matches the picture to fill in the English word at the bottom of the page.

تیز c	ورو t	پاك h
نوی d	ارزانبیه a	چتل h
لوی r	دروند a	کوچنی u
لوربیه p	ارزانبیه n	نوی o
نوی g	سیك c	کوچنی s
پاك m	زور n	ورو e

E nglish word: ◯ ◯ ◯ ◯ ◯ ◯

Find the odd one out in these groups of words.

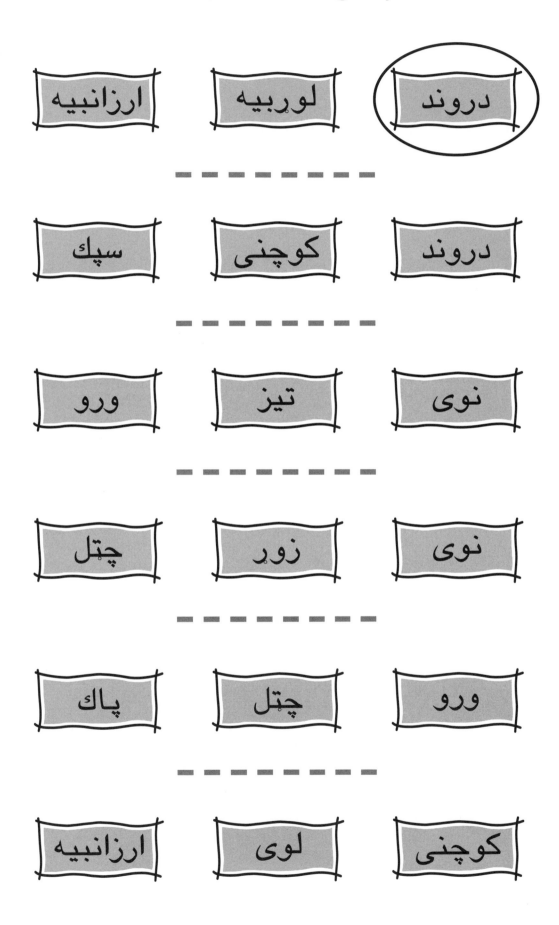

ارزانبیه	لوربیه	دروند
سپک	کوچنی	دروند
ورو	تیز	نوی
چتل	زور	نوی
پاک	چتل	ورو
ارزانبیه	لوی	کوچنی

Finally, join the English words to their Pashto opposites, as in the example.

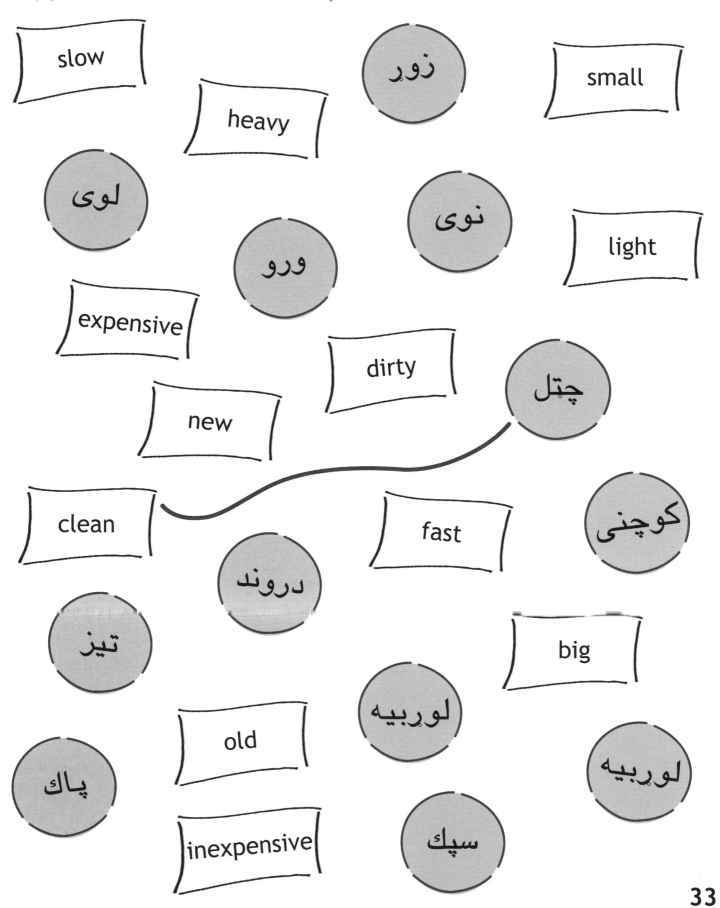

slow

زور

small

heavy

لوی

نوی

light

ورو

expensive

dirty

چتل

new

کوچنی

clean

fast

دروند

تیز

big

لوربیه

old

لوربیه

پاك

سپك

inexpensive

6 ANIMALS

Look at the pictures.
Tear out the flashcards for this topic.
Follow steps 1 and 2 of the plan in the introduction.

هـيلى *heley*

هـاتي *hateh*

پيشو *pesho*

سپى *speh*

سوى *swey*

شـادو *shado*

كب *kub*

ورى *woreh*

مـوبرك *mogak*

غوا *ghwaa*

آس *aas*

زمرى *zmareh*

© **M**atch the animals to their associated pictures, as in the example.

سوی

آس

شادو

پیشو

وری

موبرك

سپی

غوا

زمری

كب

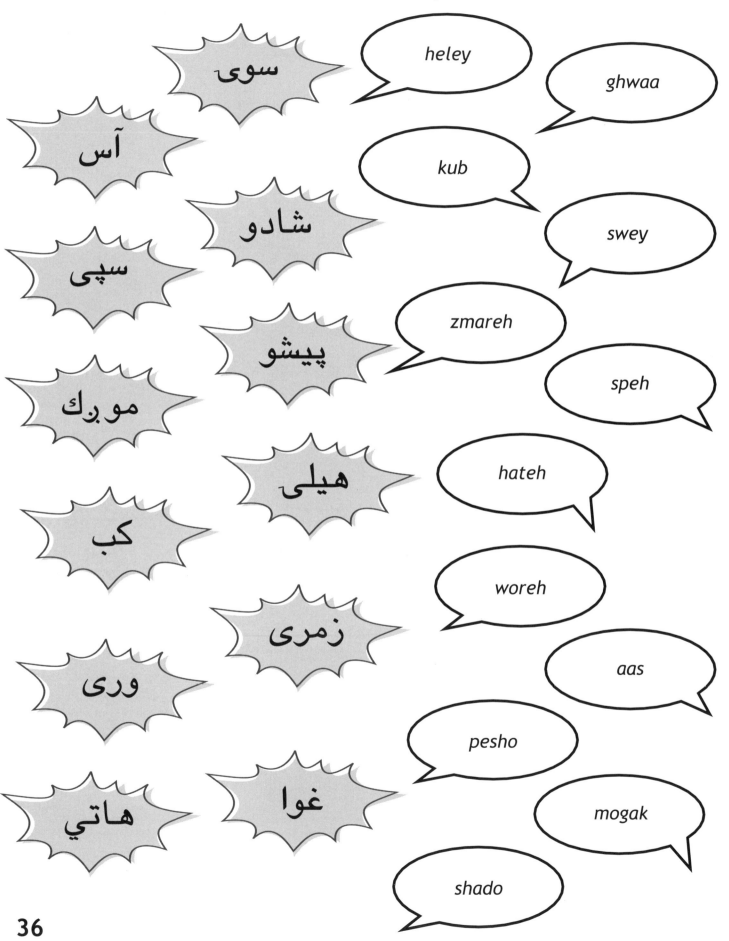

⊚ **C**heck (✔) the animal words you can find in the word pile.

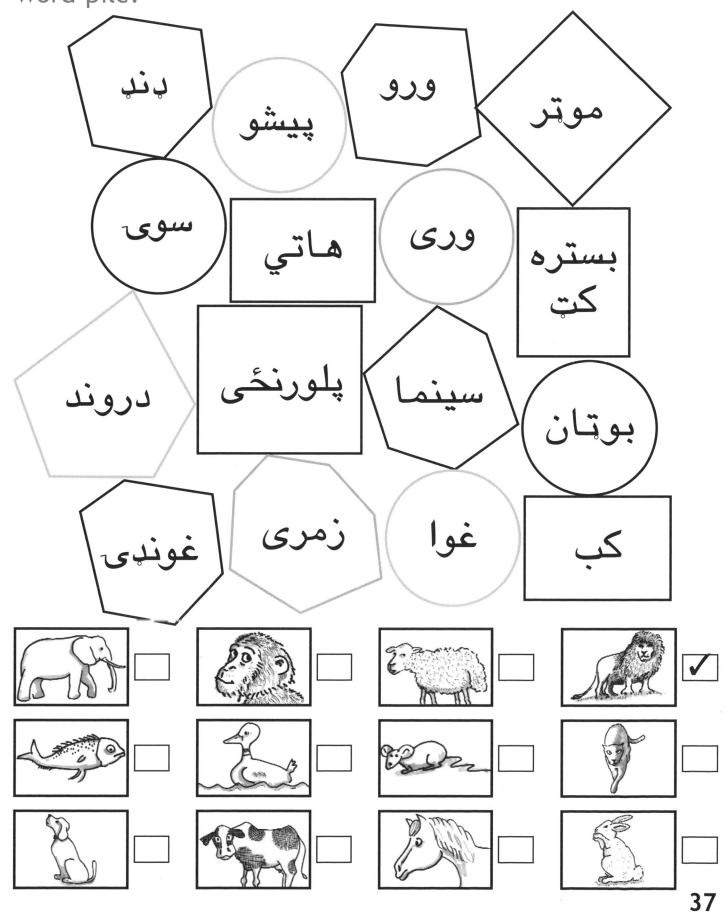

Join the Pashto animals to their English equivalents.

شادو

غوا

موږک

سپی

وری

کب

زمری

هاتي

پيشو

هيلی

سوی

آس

dog

lion

monkey

elephant

rabbit

fish

mouse

duck

cow

sheep

horse

cat

PARTS OF THE BODY

Look at the pictures of parts of the body.
Tear out the flashcards for this topic.
Follow steps 1 and 2 of the plan in the introduction.

گوته
gwota

سر *sar*

ثنگل
tsangal

سترگه *sturga*

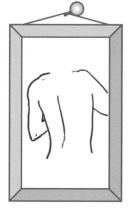
شا *shaa*

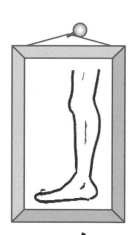
پنډی
pandey

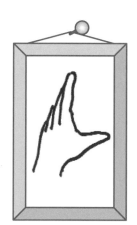
لاس *laas*

ویښتان
weshtaan

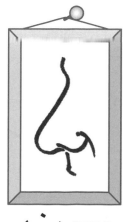
پزه *paza*

گیډه *gedda*

خوله *khoula*

غوږ
ghwag

39

Someone has ripped up the Pashto words for parts of the body. Can you join the two halves of the word again?

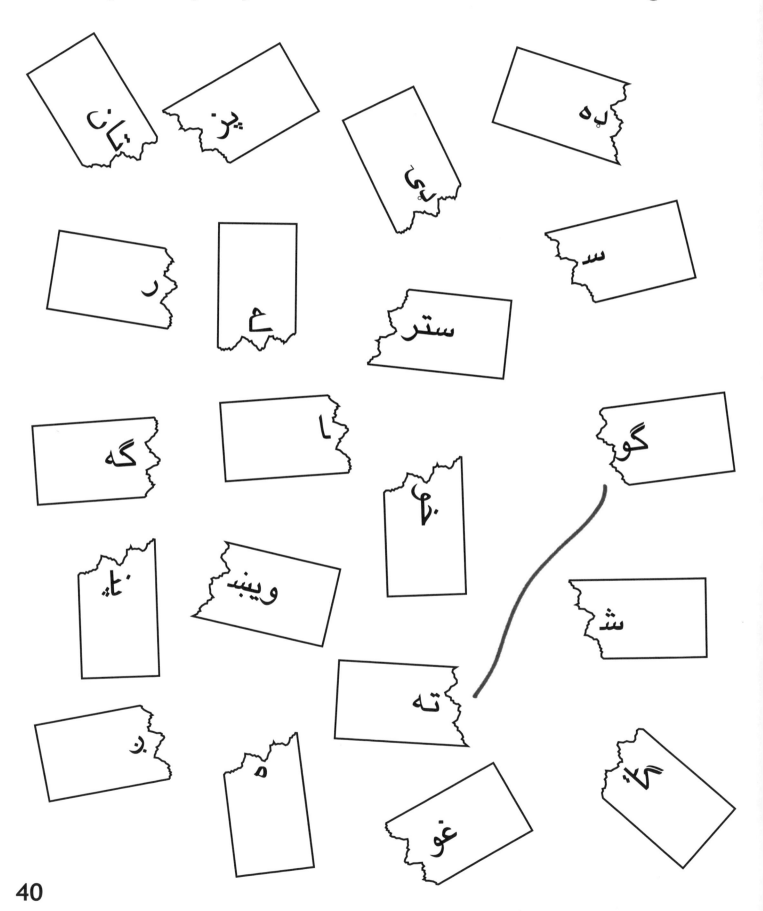

◎ **S**ee if you can find and circle six parts of the body in the word square, then draw them in the boxes below.

The words run *right* to *left*.

ه	گ	ر	ت	س	ه	گ	پ
ی	ک	غ	ه	ز	پ	ل	چ
ظ	ف	و	ت	ت	ه	ذ	حؤ
خ	غ	ه	ش	ی	ب	ذ	پ
ق	ن	ا	ت	بد	ی	و	بد
بد	غ	ی	خ	بد	و	غ	ر
م	ه	ل	و	خ	بد	س	خ
ع	غ	ظ	ز	و	ل	غ	ب

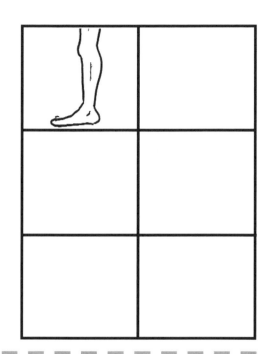

◎ **N**ow match the Pashto to the pronunciation.

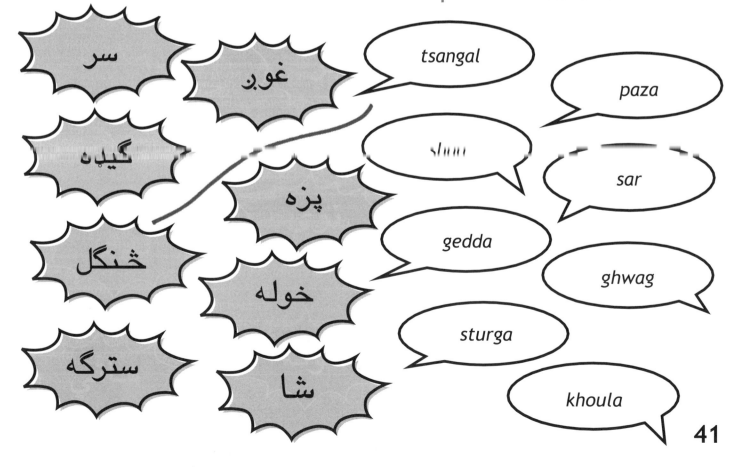

سر

غوږ

ګیډه

ثنګل

سترګه

پزه

خوله

شا

tsangal

paza

shaa

sar

gedda

ghwag

sturga

khoula

◎ Label the body with the correct number, and write the pronunciation next to the words.

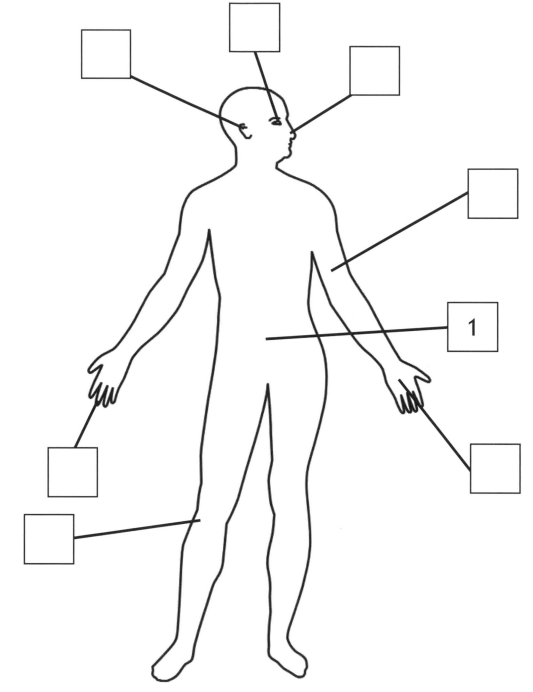

5 غوږ _____		1 گیډه _____gedda_____	
6 پنډۍ _____		2 څنگل _____	
7 سترگه _____		3 پزه _____	
8 گوته _____		4 لاس _____	

42

Finally, match the Pashto words, their pronunciation, and the English meanings, as in the example.

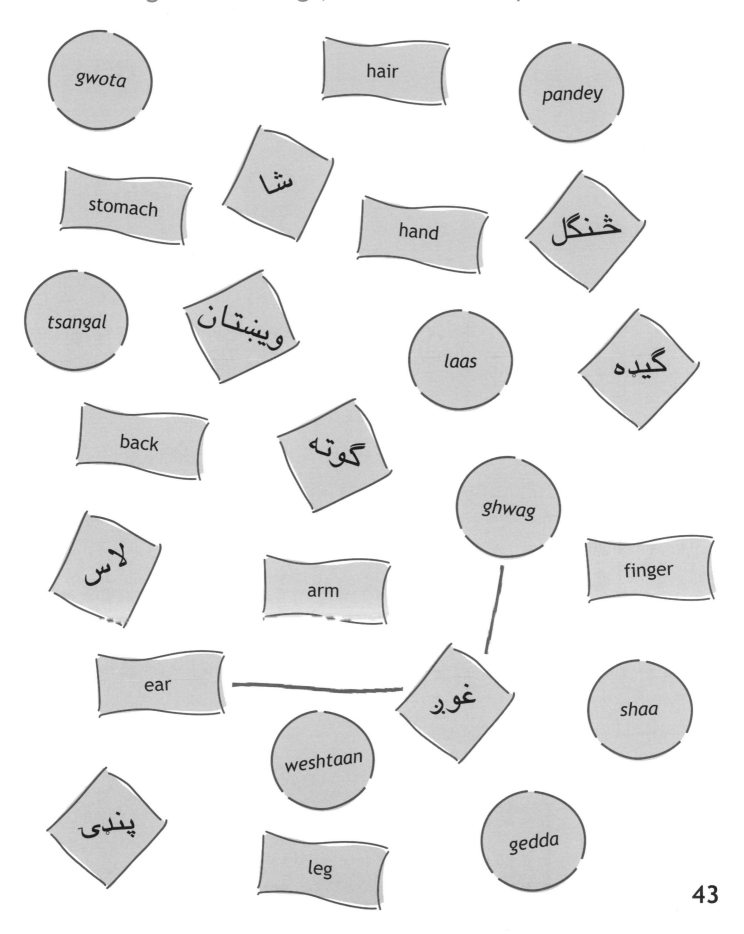

gwota

hair

pandey

stomach

شا

hand

څنګل

tsangal

وینښتان

laas

گیډه

back

ګوته

ghwag

لاس

arm

finger

ear

غوږ

shaa

weshtaan

پنډۍ

leg

gedda

⑧ USEFUL EXPRESSIONS

Look at the pictures.
Tear out the flashcards for this topic.
Follow steps 1 and 2 of the plan in the introduction.

چیرته؟ *chearta*

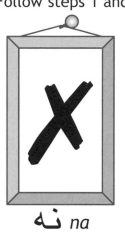

نه *na*

هو *ho*

ثنگه یی *tsanga yee*

خدای پامان *khuday paman*

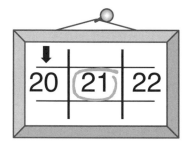

پرون *paroon*

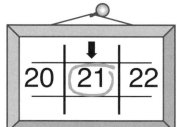

نن *nun*

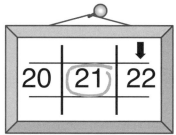

سبا *sabaa*

دلته *dulta*

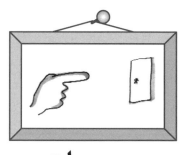

هلته *hulta*

اوس *ous*

ثومره؟ *tsomra*

وبخښنه *wabakh-kha*

عالي! *aalee*

هیله *hela*

مننه *manana*

44

Match the Pashto words to their English equivalents.

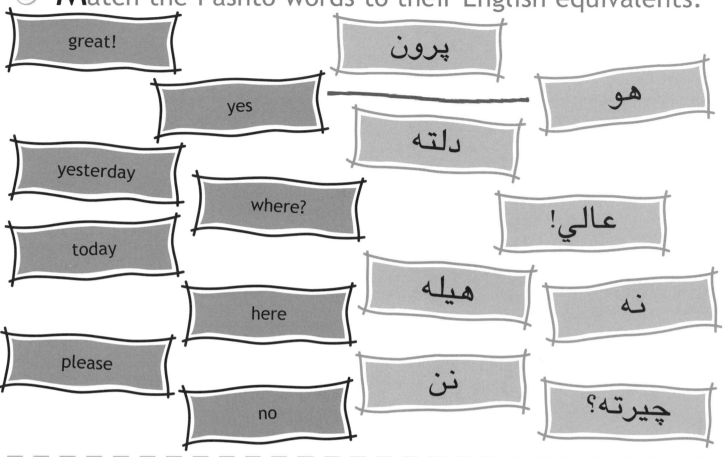

Now match the Pashto to the pronunciation.

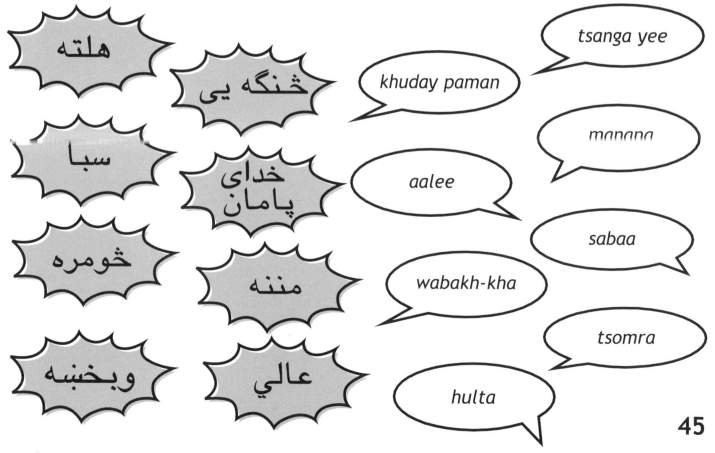

Choose the Pashto word that matches the picture to fill in the English word at the bottom of the page.

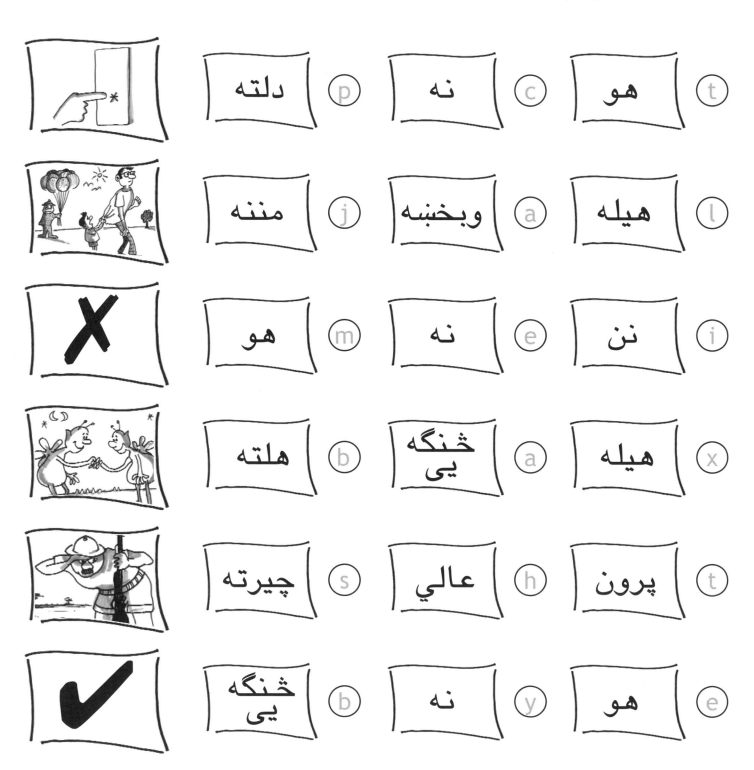

دلته ⓟ	نه ⓒ	هو ⓣ
مننه ⓙ	ويخبنه ⓐ	هيله ⓛ
هو Ⓜ	نه ⓔ	نن ⓘ
هلته ⓑ	ثنگه يی ⓐ	هيله Ⓧ
چيرته Ⓢ	عالي Ⓗ	پرون ⓣ
ثنگه يی ⓑ	نه ⓨ	هو ⓔ

Ⓔnglish word: ⓟ ◯ ◯ ◯ ◯ ◯

What are these people saying? Write the correct number in each speech bubble, as in the example.

7 چيرته	5 دلته	3 هو	1 ثنگه یی
8 ثومره	6 وبخښنه	4 نه	2 هيله

Finally, match the Pashto words, their pronunciation, and the English meanings, as in the example.

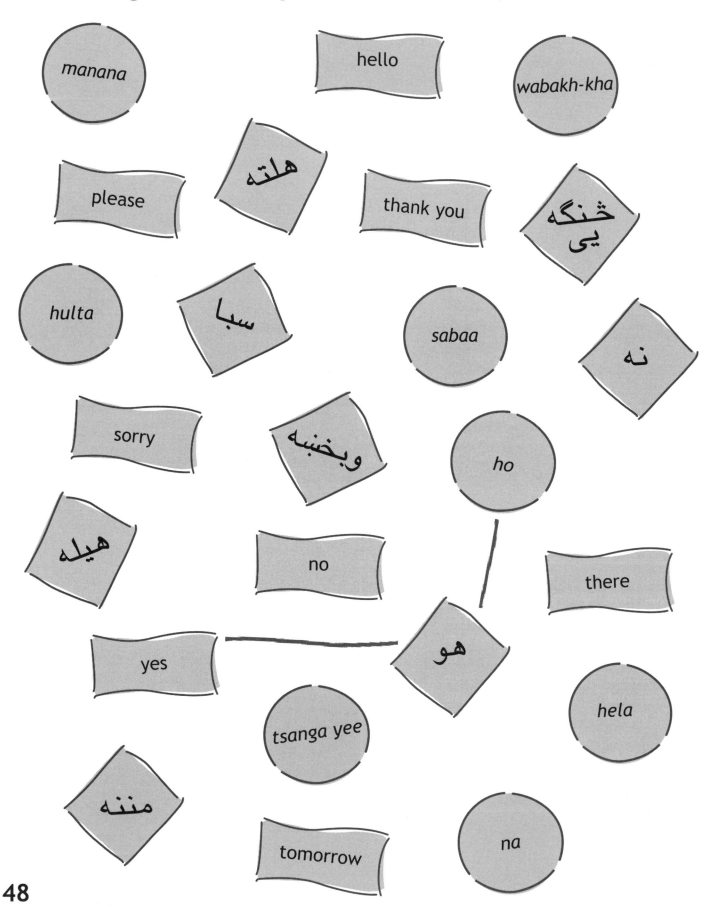

manana

hello

wabakh-kha

هلته

please

thank you

ثنگه یی

hulta

سبا

sabaa

نه

sorry

وبخښنه

ho

هیله

no

there

یس

هو

hela

تسنگه یی

مننه

na

tomorrow

48

● ROUND-UP

This section is designed to review all the 100 words you have met in the different topics. It is a good idea to test yourself with your flashcards before trying this section.

◎ These ten objects are in the picture. Can you find and circle them?

خولی	کرتی	بستره کټ	گل	دروازه
جوراب	کب	سپی	څوکی	بایسکل

See if you can remember all these words.

نن

سرویس

تیز

پزه

دبنته

هو

الماری

زمری

نبځینه کمیس

ارزانبیه

سیند

پندی

50

Find the odd one out in these groups of words and say why.

سپی	غوا	میز	شادو

Because it isn't an animal.

موټر	سرویس	اورګاډی	تیلیفون

کرونده	کرتی	نیکر	لمن

سمندر	دند	سیند	ونه

لوربیه	چتل	پاک	سینما

سوی	پیشو	کب	زمری

ثنګل	کوچ	سر	ګیده

هیله	پرون	سبا	نن

بخاری	بستره کټ	الماری	یخچال

◎ **L**ook at the objects below for 30 seconds.

◎ **C**over the picture and try to remember all the objects.
Circle the Pashto words for those you remember.

گل   بوتان   مننه   دروازه

موټر   دلته   کرتی   اورګاډی

کمربند   غر نه   آس   څوکی

جوراب   کمیس   سترګه   بستره کټ

نیکر   ټکسی   تلویزیون   شادو

Now match the Pashto words, their pronunciation, and the English meanings, as in the example.

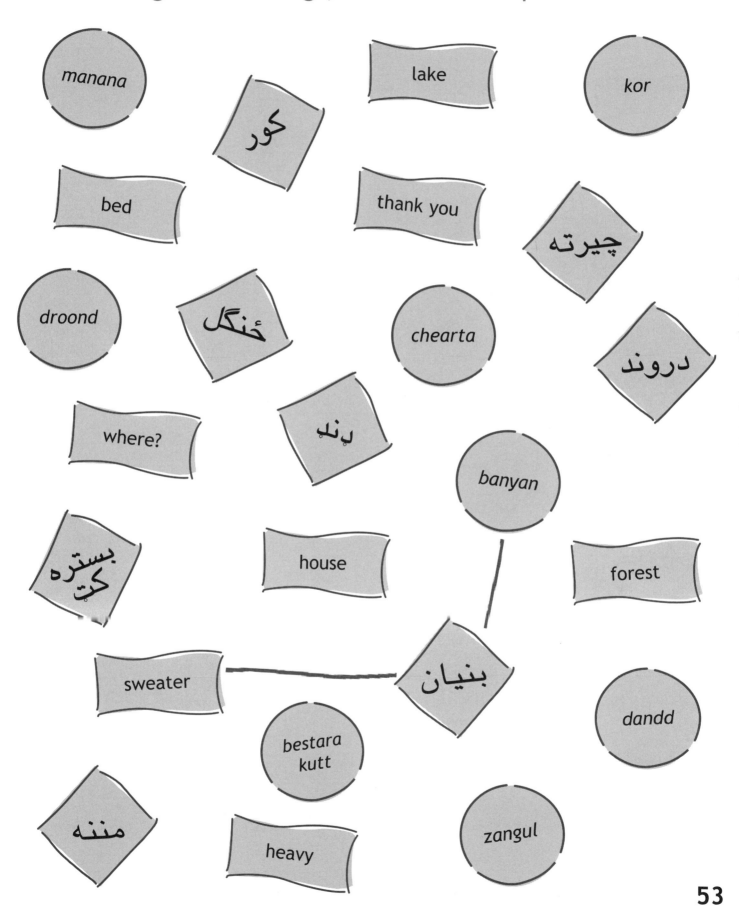

manana

lake

kor

كور

bed

thank you

چيرته

droond

څنگل

chearta

دروند

where?

ډنډ

banyan

بستره كټ

house

forest

sweater

بنيان

dandd

منثه

bestara kutt

heavy

zangul

Fill in the English phrase at the bottom of the page.

t	غوږ	g	تکسی	w	کوچ
e	پل	a	چتل	o	کرتی
i	نن	l	ثومره	m	هو
h	رستوران	l	کرکی	b	غوا
d	سپی	a	خوله	e	چیرته
v	ثنگه یی	p	میز	o	سترگه
r	سرویس	y	نه	n	غوندی
s	بخاری	e	سرک	n	سوی

English phrase:  w ◯ ◯ ◯   ◯ ◯ ◯ ◯ !

Look at the two pictures and check (✔) the objects that are different in Picture B.

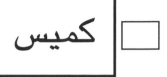

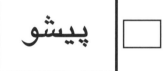

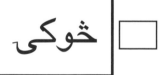

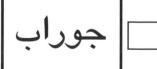

Picture A

Picture B

Now join the Pashto words to their English equivalents.

refrigerator

پانه

پانه

gidah

pants

refrigerator

store

کوچنی

school

يخچال

river

پلورنځی

great ———————— عالي

small

سيند

light

پتلون

arm

پاک

stomach

سپک

clean

آس

horse

بنوونځی

◎ **T**ry to match the Pashto to the pronunciation.

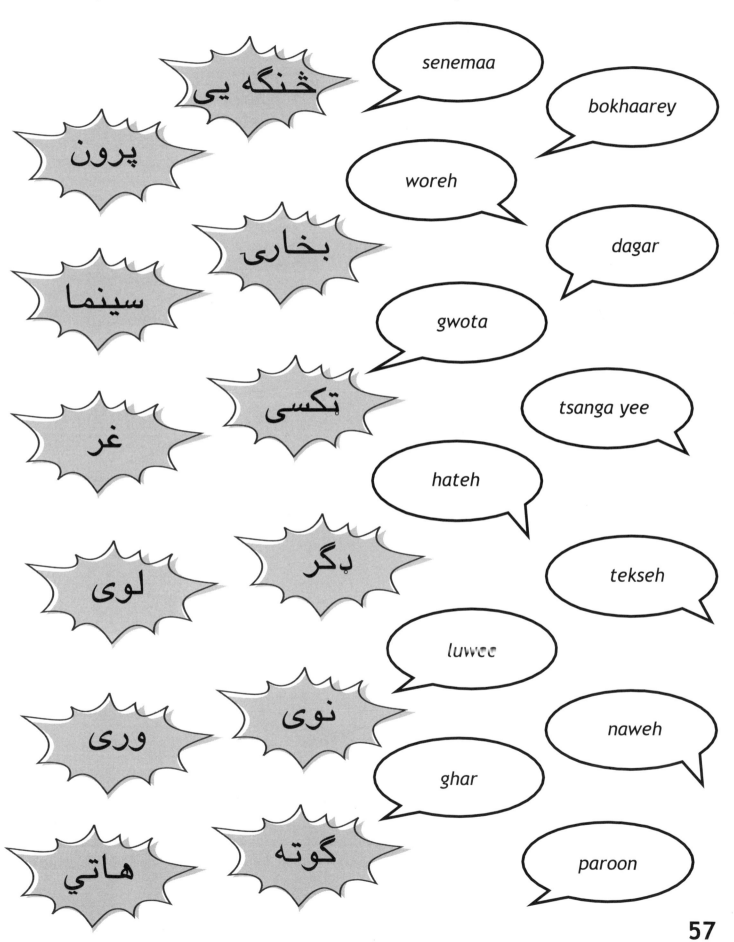

◎ Snake game.

- You will need a die and counter(s). You can challenge yourself to reach the finish or play with someone else. You have to throw the exact number to finish.

- Throw the die and move forward that number of spaces. When you land on a word you must pronounce it and say what it means in English. If you can't, you have to go back to the square you came from.

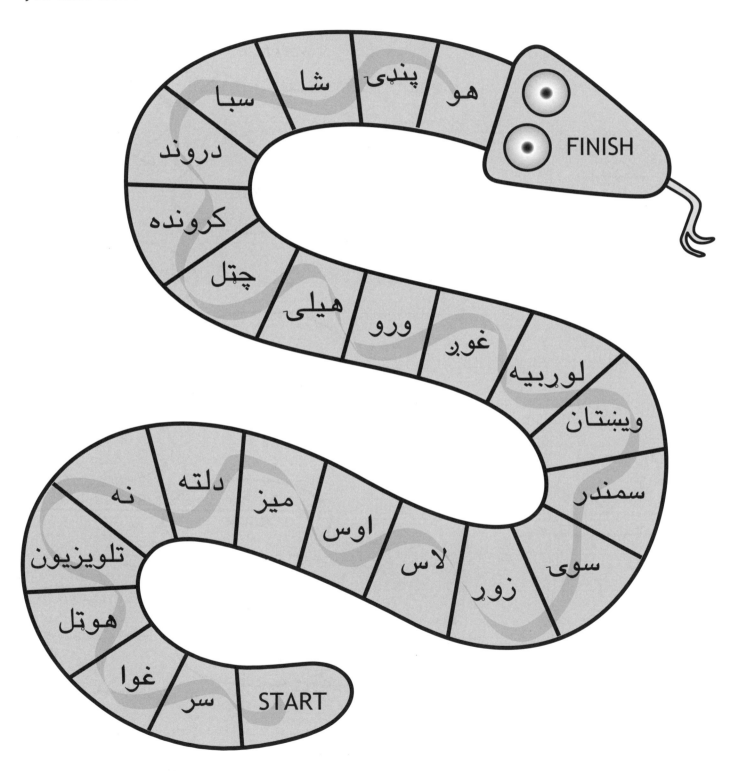

Answers

❶ AROUND THE HOME

Page 10 (top)

See page 9 for correct picture.

Page 10 (bottom)

door	دروازه
cupboard	الماری
stove	بخاری
bed	بستره کټ
table	میز
chair	څوکی
refrigerator	یخچال
computer	کمپیوتر

Page 11 (top)

میز	mez
الماری	almaarey
کمپیوتر	compeotur
بستره کټ	bestara kutt
کرکی	karrkey
تیلیفون	telefoon
تلویزیون	talvezyoon
څوکی	tsawkey

Page 11 (bottom)

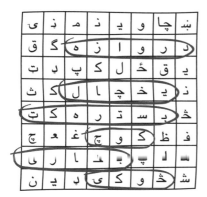

Page 12

Page 13

English word: window

❷ CLOTHES

Page 15 (top)

شنڅینه کمیس	khazena kames
نیکر	nekar
بوتان	bottaan
کمربند	kamarband
نارینه کمیس	naarena kames
کمیس	kames
خولی	khowaley
جوراب	jooraab

Page 15 (bottom)

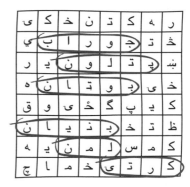

Page 16

hat	خولی	khowaley
shoe	بوتان	bottaan
sock	جوراب	jooraab
shorts	نیکر	nekar
t-shirt	کمیس	kames
belt	کمربند	kamarband
coat	کرتی	kortey
pants	پتلون	patloon

Page 17

بوتان (shoe)	2 (1 pair)
جوراب (sock)	6 (3 pairs)
بنیان (sweater)	1
کمربند (belt)	2
شنڅینه کمیس (dress)	1
نارینه کمیس (shirt)	0
کرتی (coat)	0
نیکر (shorts)	2
کمیس (t-shirt)	3
خولی (hat)	2
پتلون (pants)	0
لمن (skirt)	1

59

Page 18

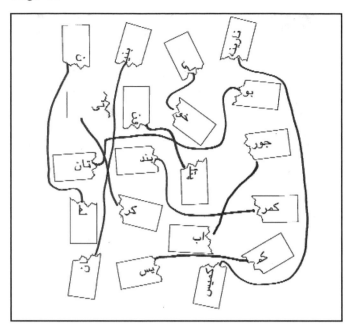

Page 22

English word: school

Page 23

سرویس	*serves*
تکسی	*tekseh*
ښوونځی	*khowanzeh*
موتر	*mottar*
هوتل	*hottel*
کور	*kor*
بایسکل	*baaysekel*
اور گاډی	*or gaaddeh*
پلورنځی	*ploranzeh*
سینما	*senemaa*
رستوران	*rustoraan*
سړک	*sarrak*

❸ AROUND TOWN

Page 20 (top)

movie theater	سینما
store	پلورنځی
hotel	هوتل
taxi	تکسی
car	موتر
train	اور گاډی
school	ښوونځی
house	کور

Page 20 (bottom)

bicycle	4
taxi	7
house	2
train	6
bus	1
road	3
car	5

Page 21

❹ COUNTRYSIDE

Page 25

See page 24 for correct picture.

Page 26

پل	✔	ډگر	✔
ونه	✔	ځنگل	✔
دښته	✘	بند	✘
غونډۍ	✘	سیند	✔
غر	✔	گل	✔
سمندر	✘	کروند	✘

Page 27 (top)

غر	*ghar*
سیند	*send*
ځنگل	*zangul*
دښته	*dakhta*
سمند	*samandar*
کروند	*karwanda*
پل	*pul*
ډگر	*dagar*

Page 27 (bottom)

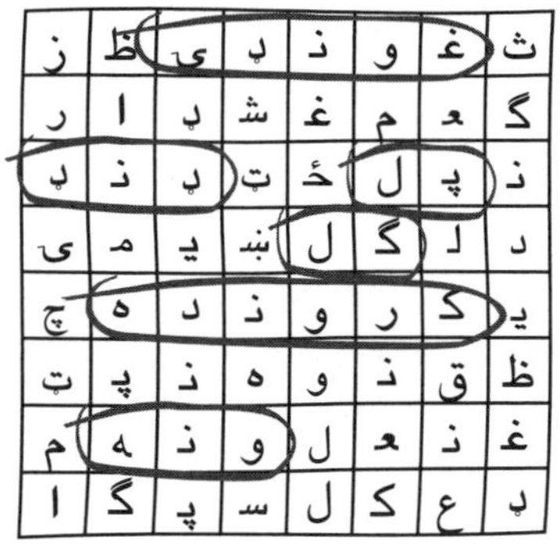

ث	غ	و	ذ	ی	د	ظ	ز
گ	ع	ش	غ	م	ا	ل	ر
ذ	پ	ل	خ	ت	ذ	ذ	پ
د	ل	گ	بـ	ی	م	د	ل
چ	ی	ک	ر	و	ذ	د	ی
ظ	ق	ذ	و	ه	ذ	پ	ت
م	ه	ذ	و	ل	ع	ذ	غ
ا	گ	پ	س	ل	ک	ع	د

Page 28

sea	سمندر	samandar
lake	ډنډ	dandd
desert	دښته	dakhta
farm	کرونده	karwanda
flower	گل	gul
mountain	غر	ghar
river	سیند	send
field	ډگر	dagar

❺ Opposites

Page 30

expensive	لوربیه
big	لوی
light	سپک
slow	ورو
clean	پاک
inexpensive	ارزانبیه
dirty	چتل
small	کوچنی
heavy	درون���
new	نوی
fast	بیر
old	زور

Page 31

English word: change

Page 32

Odd one outs are those which are not opposites:

درون��
کوچنی
نوی
چتل
ورو
ارزانبیه

Page 33

old	نوی
big	کوچنی
new	زور
slow	تیز
dirty	پاک
small	لوی
heavy	سپک
clean	چتل
light	درون��
expensive	ارزانبیه
inexpensive	لوربیه

❻ Animals

Page 35

غوا   سوی   کب    زمری

وری   سپی   شادو

آس   موږک   پیشو

Page 36

سوی	swey
آس	aas
شادو	shado
سپی	speh
پیشو	pesho
موږک	mogak
هیلی	heley
کب	kub
زمری	zmareh
وری	woreh
غوا	ghwaa
هاتي	hateh

Page 37

elephant	✔	mouse	✘
monkey	✘	cat	✔
sheep	✔	dog	✘
lion	✔	cow	✔
fish	✔	horse	✘
duck	✘	rabbit	✔

Page 38

monkey	شادو	
cow	غوا	
mouse	موږك	
dog	سپی	
sheep	وری	
fish	كب	
lion	زمری	
elephant	هاتي	
cat	پیشو	
duck	هیلی	
rabbit	سوی	
horse	آس	

❼ PARTS OF THE BODY

Page 40

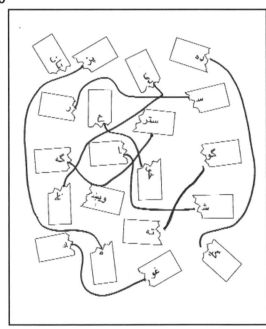

Page 41 (top)

You should have also drawn pictures of:

leg; mouth; ear; nose; eye; hair

Page 41 (bottom)

سر	sar
غوږ	ghwag
گیډه	gedda
پزه	paza
څنګل	tsangal
خوله	khoula
سترگه	sturga
شا	shaa

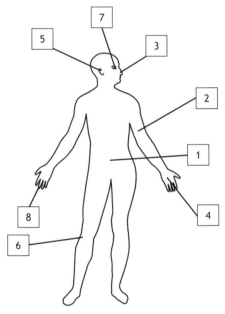

Page 42

1.	گیډه	gedda
2.	څنګل	tsangal
3.	پزه	paza
4.	لاس	laas
5.	غوږ	ghwag
6.	پنډی	pandey
7.	سترگه	sturga
8.	گوته	gwota

Page 43

ear	غوږ	ghwag
hair	ویښتان	weshtaan
hand	لاس	laas
stomach	گیډه	gedda
arm	څنګل	tsangal
back	شا	shaa
finger	گوته	gwota
leg	پنډی	pandey

8 USEFUL EXPRESSIONS

Page 45 (top)

great	عالي
yes	هو
yesterday	پرون
where?	چيرته
today	نن
here	دلته
please	هيله
no	نه

Page 45 (bottom)

هلته	hulta
څنګه يی	tsanga yee
سبا	sabaa
خدای پامان	khuday paman
څومره	tsomra
مننه	manana
وبخښه	wabakh-kha
عالي	aalee

Page 46

English word: please

Page 47

Page 48

yes	هو	ho
hello	څنګه يی	tsanga yee
no	نه	na
sorry	وبخښه	wabakh-kha
please	هيله	hela
there	هلته	hulta
thank you	مننه	manana
tomorrow	سبا	sabaa

● ROUND-UP

Page 49

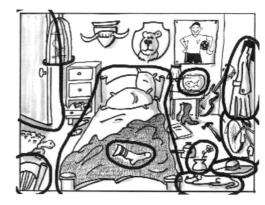

Page 50

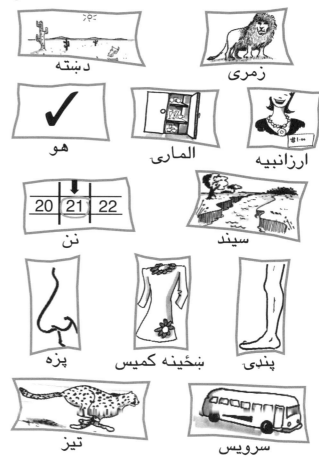

Page 51

ميز (Because it isn't an animal.)

تيليفون (Because it isn't a means of transportation.)

کرونده (Because it isn't an item of clothing.)

ونه (Because it isn't connected with water.)

سينما (Because it isn't a descriptive word.)

کب (Because it lives in water/doesn't have legs.)

کوچ (Because it isn't a part of the body.)

هيله (Because it isn't an expression of time.)

بستره کټ (Because you wouldn't find it in
the kitchen.)

63

Page 52

Words that appear in the picture:

كميس
موتر
گل
بوتان
اور گادی
شادو
تلويزيون
څوکۍ
كمربند
نيكر

Page 53

sweater	بنيان	banyan
lake	دند	dandd
thank you	مننه	manana
bed	بستره كټ	bestara kutt
house	كور	kor
forest	ځنگل	zangul
where?	چيرته	chearta
heavy	دروند	droond

Page 54

English phrase: well done!

Page 55

Script	Mark	
نيكر	✔	(shade)
كميس	✗	
دروازه	✔	(handle)
پيشو	✗	
څوكۍ	✔	(back)
كب	✔	(direction)
جوراب	✔	(pattern)
سپی	✗	

Page 56

refrigerator	يخچال
pants	پتلون
store	پلورنځی
school	ښوونځی
river	سيند
great	عالي
small	كوچنی
light	سپك
arm	څنگل
stomach	گيډه
clean	پاك
horse	آس

Page 57

څنگه یی	tsanga yee
پرون	paroon
بخاری	bokhaarey
سينما	senemaa
تكسی	tekseh
غر	ghar
دگر	dagar
لوی	luwee
نوی	naweh
وری	woreh
گوته	gwota
هاتي	hateh

Page 58

Here are the English equivalents of the word, in order from START to FINISH:

head	sar	hair	weshtaan
cow	ghwaa	expensive	lowarrbaya
hotel	hottel	ear	ghwag
television	talvezyoon	slow	wro
no	na	duck	heley
here	dulta	dirty	chattel
table	mez	farm	karwanda
now	ous	heavy	droond
hand	laas	tomorrow	sabaa
old	zoorr	back	shaa
rabbit	swey	leg	pandey
sea	samandar	yes	ho

کمپیوتر	کرکی
compeotur	*karrkey* ✂
میز	الماری
mez	*almaarey*
یخچال	څوکی
yakhchaal	*tsawkey*
کوچ	بخاری
kawch	*bokhaarey*
دروازه	بستره کټ
darwaaza	*bestara kutt*
تیلیفون	تلویزیون
telefoon	*talvezyoon*

window	computer
cupboard	table
chair	refrigerator
stove	sofa
bed	door
television	telephone

کمربند	کرتی
kamarband	*kortey*
لمن	خولی
laman	*khowaley*
کمیس	بوتان
kames	*bottaan*
بنیان	نارینه کمیس
banyan	*naarena kames*
نیکر	جوراب
nekar	*jooraab*
پتلون	بنځینه کمیس
patloon	*khazena kames*

coat	belt
hat	skirt
shoe	t-shirt
shirt	sweater
sock	shorts
dress	pants

موتر

motta

ښوونځی

khowanzeh

سینما

senemad

سرك

sarrak

پلورنځی

ploranzeh

هوټل

hottel

بایسکل

baayseke

تکسی

tekseh

سرویس

serves

رستوران

rustoraan

کور

kor

اور گاډی

or gaaddeh

car	school
movie theater	road
store	hotel
bicycle	taxi
bus	restaurant
house	train

ځنګل	دنډ
zangu	*dandd*
سمندر	غوندۍ
samanda	*ghonddey*
ونه	غر
wund	*ghar*
ګل	د ښته
gu	*dakhta*
سیند	پل
send	*pul*
ډګر	کرونده
daga	*karwanda*

forest	lake
sea	hill
tree	mountain
flower	desert
river	bridge
field	farm

درورند	سپك
droond	*spak*
لوی	كوچنی
luwee	*kochneh*
زور	نوی
zoorr	*naway*
تیز	ورو
teaz	*wro*
پاك	چټل
paak	*chattel*
ارزانبیه	لوربیه
arzaanbaya	*lowarrbaya*

light	heavy
small	big
new	old
slow	fast
dirty	clean
expensive	inexpensive

پیشو	هیلی
pesho	*heley*
غوا	موبرك
ghwa	*mogak*
سپی	سوی
speh	*swey*
شادو	آس
shad	*aas*
کب	زمری
kub	*zmareh*
وری	هاتي
woreh	*hateh*

cat	duck
cow	mouse
dog	rabbit
monkey	horse
fish	lion
sheep	elephant

ثنگل *tsangal*	گوته *gwot...*
سر *sar*	خوله *khoul...*
غوږ *ghwag*	پنډۍ *pandey...*
لاس *laas*	گیډه *gedd...*
سترگه *sturga*	وینستان *weshtaar...*
پزه *paza*	شا *shad...*

finger	arm
mouth	head
leg	ear
stomach	hand
hair	eye
back	nose

مننه *manan*	هیله *hela*
نه *na*	هو *ho*
خدای پامان *khuday pamar*	څنګه یی *tsanga yee*
نن *nun*	پرون *paroon*
چیرته؟ *chearta*	سبا *sabaa*
هلته *hulta*	دلته *dulta*
څومره؟ *tsomra*	وبخښنه! *wabakh-kha*
اوس *ous*	عالي! *aalee*

thank you	please
no	yes
goodbye	hello
today	yesterday
where?	tomorrow
there	here
how much?	sorry!
now	great!